1

MARY, QUEEN OF PEACE

This book is dedicated to the six young people:

Vida (Vicka) Ivanković, born September 3, 1964
Mirjana Dragicević, born March 18, 1965
Marija Pavlović, born April 1, 1965
Ivan Dragicević, born May 25, 1965
Ivanka Ivanković, born June 21, 1966
Jakov Colo, born May 6, 1971

MARY, QUEEN OF PEACE

Is the Mother of God Appearing in Medjugorje?

Lucy Rooney SND
Robert Faricy SJ

ALBA · HOUSE   NEW · YORK

SOCIETY OF ST. PAUL, 2187 VICTORY BLVD., STATEN ISLAND, NEW YORK 10314

First published in 1984 by Veritas Publications, 7-8 Lower Abbey Street, Dublin 1, Ireland.

Photos on pages 14, 80 and 98 by Luigi Bianchi from "Medjugorje," ed. Marelli di Como (Italy).

ISBN 0-8189-0475-5

Designed, printed and bound in the United States of America by the Fathers and Brothers of the Society of St. Paul, 2187 Victory Boulevard, Staten Island, New York 10314, as part of their communications apostolate.

---

1 2 3 4 5 6 7 8 9 (Current Printing: first digit).

Contents

Foreword

In this book we have tried to give an account of the reported apparitions of the Blessed Virgin Mary in a small village in the hills of central Yugoslavia. As we write this, the apparitions continue every day. Because we write of something that still goes on, and because there has as yet been no ecclesiastical or scientific investigation of the matter, our account takes the form not of a formal study or examination but of a report of the personal experience of two people, of two pilgrims. We have both been blessed by the Lord by our visits to the village where the Mother of God appears every day to a small group of young people and we want to share with you what we have seen and heard. We are both convinced of the authenticity of these appearances of Our Lady but of course we leave all final judgments to Church authorities. This said, in the chapters that follow we have described the appearances as factual rather than continually refer to them as "reported" or "alleged." The reader will understand that this wording reflects a shared personal opinion pending the outcome of the Church's official investigation. We want to thank Archbishop Frane Franić of Split, Bishop Pavao Zanić and the Rev. Dr. Ante Brajko of Mostar for their hospitality to Father Faricy during his visits to Yugoslavia. We also thank Father Tom Forrest CSSR and Sister Mary O'Duffy SMG, for their help and encouragement; Father Francis A. Sullivan SJ for reading the text and suggesting changes and Leslie Wearne who typed the manuscript and helped us in other ways.

We are especially grateful to Father Tomislav Vlasić OFM, to Sister Janja Boras OFM, to the other Franciscan priests and sisters of St. James Parish, Medjugorje, Bosnia-Herzegovina, Yugoslavia and to Vicka, Mirjana, Ivan, Ivanka, Marija, and Jakov.

Lucy Rooney SND
Robert Faricy SJ
Rome, Italy
The Feast of Mary, Mother of God

MARY, QUEEN OF PEACE

I

A First Visit to Medjugorje

By Robert Faricy SJ

In the autumn of 1981 a popular Italian magazine carried an article on alleged appearances of the Blessed Virgin Mary in southern Yugoslavia, in the village of Medjugorje in the mountains of Bosnia-Herzegovina. The article made me decide to go to Medjugorje to investigate. Here, then, is an account of my trip, made from notes I took on the way.

Going to Medjugorje

Shortly after leaving Trieste, the train stops at the Italian-Yugoslav border. I have been told that if I give any sign I intend to go to Medjugorje, the Yugoslavian border police will turn me back. Accordingly, I have my copies of the Italian magazine article hidden in an inside pocket and no telltale religious literature in my small bag. Sure enough, after the Italian customs agents have chatted with me and complimented me on my Italian, the Yugoslavian policeman checks my bag thoroughly. He finds a book. Holding it gingerly between thumb and forefinger, he brandishes it triumphantly before me. 'Vat iss dis book?' he says with suspicion and menace. I explain that it is a guidebook to Italy; but he checks the book carefully to verify my words.

The train arrives in Split early the next day. I look for an older priest there with whom I have corresponded and who I hope will direct me to Medjugorje. I have lost his address, so I go to the cathedral in the center of Split to ask where I might find him. The beautiful cathedral, in the heart of the old medieval city, has all its doors locked. I follow my ears to the source of children singing and in a basement room of a building adjoining the cathedral, a nun writes an address for me on a slip of paper.

Eventually I find the priest, but he tells me I cannot go to Medjugorje alone. It is too far and there is no public transport. Then he turns on the radio. "They watch us and listen to us all the time," he explains; the radio will cover our voices. Then he tells me that if I go to Medjugorje alone I would be spotted as a foreigner before I ever arrived. Once the authorities knew my destination, I would be immediately ushered to the nearest border. The Church, he continues, is under severe attack from the government and has been since the death of Tito. In Croatia especially, the government fears the Church. Not that all the Croatians are practicing Catholics. In Split, less than twenty percent of those baptized practice their faith. In the country, the percentage of practicing Catholics varies and can go as high as ninety percent.

Map of the area around Medjugorje

I insist that, somehow, I will go to Medjugorje. The priest arranges a car and a driver for me and the driver and I leave that afternoon for a three-hour drive in the rain. The village of Medjugorje lies about twelve miles west of Mostar in the republic of Bosnia-Herzegovina. In this area, the people are almost all Croatian and strongly Catholic.

We arrive at the Medjugorje parish church a little after five; the church is already full, even though Mass does not begin until six. Most of the people, more than a thousand, have walked miles in the rain. I count only seven cars in the parking lot. The driver tells me this happens every night but even more people come on weekends.

I begin to enter the church where some of the young people who have seen the Blessed Virgin Mary are leading the rosary. But the driver takes my arm and leads me to the side door of the rectory, where a Franciscan friar meets us. "What do you want?" he asks me suspiciously. "Why have you come?" Almost immediately, three other Franciscan priests and two sisters join us in the hallway, all of them clearly overworked and nervous. We speak briefly, finding common languages and suddenly a door opens and the pastor walks in, takes my hand, and says my name. To my surprise, he is a man I know, Tomislav Vlasic. In contrast to the others his face wears an expression of great serenity. He wants to prepare for Mass, he tells me; he invites me to concelebrate with him and says we will meet in the sacristy. When the devotions after Mass finish, he continues, we can talk. And we do talk, into the night. Father Vlasic tells me the story.

What is happening at Medjugorje?

On the afternoon of June 24, 1981 on the hill of Podbrdo on Mount Crnica in Bijabovici in the parish of Medjugorje, a lady dressed in grey and wearing a white veil appeared in the air to some young people. In the days following, the six young people returned late every afternoon to the hill and the Blessed Virgin continued to appear and to speak with them almost every day. The lady spoke of peace and asked them to pray and do penance for peace in the world; to go to the sacraments frequently and to have confidence in God.

Soon, most of the people in the area knew what was happening, word spread and large crowds began to assemble every afternoon on the hill to pray and to wait for Our Lady to appear to the six young persons.

The village of Medjugorje

There were miracles; a blind man now sees, a paralyzed child walks, many who were sick are healed. Hundreds of conversions took place. Enemies were reconciled. But the greatest miracle was, and is, the religious awakening of the region around Medjugorje, the spirit of prayer and the fact that almost everyone fasts regularly on bread and water.

The local Communist government, its seat at the nearby city of Citluk, became alarmed, particularly because so many young people went up on the hill every evening to say the rosary and other prayers. Special evening events, held under government auspices for young people, dances and films, attracted only a handful of the local youth; they were almost all up on the hill.

After only a short time the government began to take serious repressive measures. At first, no cars were allowed to enter Medjugorje in late afternoon or evening. Then the local police gave orders to the pastor that no religious assemblies could take place outside the church; the praying on the hill moved down into the parish church. "We have the best Communist government in the world," a Franciscan informs me laughing, "they tell our people to go to church." The six young people to whom Mary continued to appear were arrested and taken to the police station, threatened seriously, told to recant and then released. The pastor was notified that he would have to cease this religious nonsense and stop fooling the people. Over fifty persons have been arrested and held for at least some time in connection with the appearances at Medjugorje. A few have been sentenced to long prison terms.

Podbrdo hill, scene of the first apparition on June 24, 1981

Publicity has come almost entirely from the national Communist newspapers, which have viciously attacked the events at Medjugorje, labeling the Franciscan priests and sisters "separatists" and linking them to an extreme right wing Nazi-Fascist group called the Ustaski Movement. Ustaski aims at Croatian independence through violent means. Apparently composed of a few fanatics, its recent activities have been limited to symbolic gestures such as hijacking a plane. A cartoon in a national paper shows the Blessed Virgin dressed as a terrorist, a large knife held between her teeth, appearing to some children. The caption reads: "The true face of the Blessed Mother." The attacks in the press and the ludicrous charges of sedition and terrorism have called nationwide attention to Medjugorje in a way that the Catholic press could never have done.

The appearances have continued, Father Tomislav Vlasic tells me. The Blessed Virgin has continued to appear to and to speak with each of the young people every day, even though they are not together. Apparently she has been forming each one personally in the spiritual life.

Mass at Medjugorje

The young people have now finished leading the congregation in saying the rosary and the pastor and I meet in the sacristy to vest for Mass. On important feast days, such as the Immaculate Conception on December 8, over ten thousand people come for the evening Mass. Most of them have to stand outside the church to participate as best they can. I have been told that the congregation holds at least eight or ten plainclothes policemen every night; I peek out of the sacristy door but all I see is an ocean of faces.

The Mass lasts a long time. The homily, preached by Father Vlasic with great force and fervor, goes over twenty minutes. Everyone goes to Communion. I am impressed by the attention, by the deep spirit of reverence in the silences and also in the singing.

After Mass, no one leaves. Those of the six young people remaining in Medjugorje lead the congregation in saying the Our Father, Hail Mary, and Glory Be seven times. The pastor, Father Vlasic, says a long prayer for healing. He prays at the altar, facing the

Ivan, Marija, Ivanka, a friend, Jakov and Vicka during the recitation of the rosary

congregation, arms extended over them for the healing of their bodies, their hearts, their relationships. During the long prayer, no one moves or shuffles feet or coughs.

When the prayer for healing has finished, most of the congregation leave. The few who remain come up to the altar, into the sanctuary, to be prayed over individually for various kinds of healing. We form little groups of two and three to listen briefly to the troubles of those who want prayers and then to pray over them simply for their intentions. The strong spirit of reverence, even of awe, remains in the church. The praying in small groups takes place quietly, reverently, very gently.

What are they like, the six young people, to whom the Blessed Virgin appears and speaks every day? They seem completely normal, even average. They look and dress like young people do all over the world. Looking at them I could easily think they were American or French or Australian. They obviously have great love for and trust in their spiritual director, Father Tomislav Vlasic. About forty years old, Father Vlasic possesses a great serenity. He is warm, kind and forceful; most of all, he is peacefully courageous. He could be sent to prison for a long term. He is not afraid, but he is careful. "I base my preaching entirely on the Bible and on sound theology" he tells me. He makes no references whatever to politics, to political currents, events or possibilities.

A Personal Evaluation

How can I evaluate my experience at Medjugorje? It was a time of great grace for me personally although I find it difficult to say why or to describe in any way what my trip meant for my personal relationship with God, for my spiritual life. Certainly, I feel closer to Mary, more aware of her loving motherliness in my life. I know that, somehow, I *am* closer to her than I was.

How do I judge what has happened and what is still going on at Medjugorje? The Church has not yet spoken officially and like any Catholic I will conform my personal evaluation to the Church's authoritative pronouncement when that comes. Personally and subjectively, I have no doubts as to the validity of the apparitions. Any doubts I might have had were removed by what I saw and heard, especially by the powerful spirit of holiness, reverence and prayer. If I needed any confirmation from outside sources, I had that confirmation from the older priest in Split who lent me his car, from the positive evaluation of a respected priest teacher of spiritual theology in Zagreb and from the ferocious and brutal Communist opposition.

If the Blessed Virgin really has appeared and spoken to the six young people and if she really has continued to do so, then surely the events at Medjugorje have an importance perhaps even greater than those of Lourdes and Fatima. The story of Medjugorje is far from over. There are no facilities yet for pilgrimages and the Franciscan staff remains small and overworked. Of course, the Church has not yet officially investigated the situation and passed judgment on it. It seems inevitable to me that Medjugorje will become an international Marian shrine, in spite of the opposition of the Communist government.

A year after my first visit to Medjugorje, I went again with Sister Lucy Rooney SND, and Father Tom Forrest CSSR. We stayed several days and spent much of our time interviewing Father Tomislav Vlasic and the young people to whom the Blessed Virgin was still appearing daily. The following two chapters are, to a large extent, based on our notes from the visit, as well as on a manuscript written by Father Svetozar Kraljevic OFM to whom Sister Lucy and I are grateful.

Vicka, Jakov and Ivanka in rapt attention during one of the apparitions

II

The Story of Mary's Appearances

By Lucy Rooney SND

June 1981

The parish church of St. James, Medjugorje, serves five villages which in all have about five hundred and thirty families. In one of the villages, Bijakovici, on a summer afternoon, June 24, 1981, two girls set off for a walk. Fifteen-year-old Ivanka lives in Mostar but her family has a house and land in Bijakovici. Her friend, Mirjana, sixteen years old, lives at Sarajevo but spends the summer with her grandmother in Bijakovici. The two girls decided to walk in the direction of Podbrdo hill ("under-hill"). Ivanka describes what happened.

Mirjana and I were at my house and then we went for a walk. As we returned I looked towards the hill and I saw a shining figure, like Our Lady. I said to Mirjana: "Look! Our Lady." She didn't even look but motioned with her hand, saying, "Come on, Our Lady wouldn't appear to us." Then we came to Milka's house (the young sister of Marija). She asked us to bring the sheep home. We went back, talking and then we saw Our Lady. We knelt down and prayed there. The sheep went home; we chased them.

Vicka Ivankovic, seventeen years old, had been to school in Citluk that morning and was lying down resting. Ivanka and Mirjana had left a message for her saying, "As soon as you get up, come to Jakov's house." Vicka, still wearing slippers, went to look for them for, as she said, "Every summer we are together all the time."

Vicka describes what happened:

When I reached the road where they were, I saw they were waving and calling me to come. When I arrived up there, Mirjana said, "Look up there—Our Lady." I did not even look—did not have the time. I left my slippers and ran away barefoot. That was on the dirt and rock road. As I ran, I met Ivan Dragicevic and Ivan Ivankovic. They were picking apples and asked me if I wanted some. I said, "No"—and then, "Ivan, Our Lady! They say she is appearing up there. Come with me; I'm afraid." He, Ivan Dragicevic, sixteen years old—said, "What are you afraid of? Let's go."

I thought he wasn't afraid, but when we arrived and I turned to ask him: "Do you see anything?" he was already gone; I saw him running away. Ivan Ivankovic stayed. I asked him if he saw anything; he said he saw something completely white, moving. Milka, who was with us, said, "I see Our Lady."

It was now after six-thirty, raining a little and getting dark. I saw her about two hundred meters away—a really white figure, a gown, dark hair. Then she called us to come. We said to each other: "She is calling us"—but who would go? I went home before the others, with little Milka. We went to her sister, Marija, and told her we had seen Our Lady on the hill. She just laughed and did not want to talk about it. But the other people teased us saying: "You should have caught her." My sister said: "That was a flying saucer." But we did not pay any attention. Let them talk.

The following day, most of these young people were at work in the tobacco fields. They finished as early as they could, except Milka, whose mother gave her an extra job, saying: "Let Marija go, that is enough."

Vicka, Jakov, Ivanka and Marija during one of the apparitions

Sixteen-year-old Marija, seeing Ivan Dragicevic, Vicka, Mirjana and Ivanka leaving for the hills, said to them: "I would like just to be there if you see Our Lady, even if I don't see her." They promised to call Marija and ten-year-old Jakov. Ivan Ivankovic did not go that second day thinking that it was childish to go to the hill for some vision or other. Several other children and two adults followed them. Vicka takes up the story.

> It was about six o'clock. Mirjana and myself were walking together, talking. Ivanka was first, walking ahead of us. Suddenly she called: "Look! Our Lady!" It was still day, I was able to see her, the face, eyes, hair, gown, everything. We were down on the road and did not know what to do. I went to call Marija and Jakov. They came immediately. Our Lady called us to come up. Looking from the bottom of the hill, it seems close, but it is not. We were running at great speed. It was not like walking on the ground—we did not look for the pathway—we simply ran in the direction where she was. It was like being pulled up into the air. I was afraid. We were there in five minutes and though I was barefoot, no thorn hurt me.

The adults who were there confirm this. They were amazed at the speed and unable to keep up. Vicka continued:

> When we were about two meters from Our Lady, we felt we were taken and dropped to our knees. Jakov knelt in a thorn bush. I thought, "He will be hurt," but he came out of it unharmed. Marija at first only saw

something white but gradually it came clearer and she saw like the rest of us. Jakov said, "I see Our Lady."

Ivanka was the first to speak. Her mother had died two months earlier and she asked about her. Our Lady said she was with her, was well and that Ivanka was not to worry. Ivanka says that not knowing what to do, they were "praying a little, crying a little." They prayed the Hail Mary and Our Father.

The adults present witness that the children's heads turned as one, in the direction that the figure went, soaring, the children said, into the air.

Since that day these four girls and two boys say that they have seen the Mother of God every day (with a few exceptions) around six in the evening. Mirjana's daily visions ceased on Christmas Day 1982. The others' continue.

Crowds Gather

On the third evening, June 26, 1981, a thousand or more people streamed towards the hillside. A neighbor of the children, Marinko Ivankovic, was there for the first time. Marinko lives at Bijakovici with his wife, three children and his parents. He works as a mechanic at Citluk and first heard the news from Vicka and Marija when he gave them a ride in his car to their classes on June 25. On the third evening he was there to protect the six children from the crowd. Marinko says:

I will tell you about it. I am a practicing Catholic and I attend the marriage encounter weekends. There is a second reason—I am concerned about the circumstances of these children. Ivanka—her mother is dead, her father is in Germany an emigrant worker; Vicka's father is in Germany; Jakov's father lives in Bosnia and rarely visits; Mirjana's family lives in Sarajevo. Someone had to protect them, to give them strength.

Marinko and the six young people decided to get together at the place at the foot of the hill where they were on the first evening. As they stood together, a beam of brilliant light passed three times over the village and the area. Many who were present saw it. When asked later by the pastor: "Is there anything that leads you there?" Jakov said "We see a light, then Our Lady, and we go!"

This evening, the place to which the light drew them was about three hundred yards away from that of the other two evenings. Marinko describes how the crowd of a thousand or more ran as best they could, a long way over steep, wet ground. Marinko had to help the girls as they staggered over the rocks. He writes:

Ivan and Jakov went first and then the girls and myself. I was observing Ivan closely. He seemed to be looking about as though he had lost something. Then he suddenly ran towards the northeast. When I turned towards the girls, they were gone too. The next moment I saw them kneeling together near a stone with some green around it. I called out: "Is she there?" "Yes," they answered. The way they were acting at the time impressed me, convinced me.

Vicka had brought holy water which she sprinkled, saying: "If you are Our Lady, stay with us, if you are not, begone." The lady smiled—beautifully.

Marinko had told the six to ask the lady why she had come. She replied: "I came because there are many good believers here. I want to be with you, to convert and to reconcile everyone." As on each evening, she said as she left, "Go in God's peace." The children saw the sky lit with stars, though it was still daylight.

It was a late June afternoon when the heat and the number of people pressing close to them overcame Ivanka, Mirjana and Vicka and they all fainted. There was chaos until Marinko and his friends formed a circle around them. They had been speaking with Our Lady for thirty minutes. After the first ten, she had indicated that they should get up from their knees off the stony ground.

As they were helped from the hill, Marija, who looks the most frail but who had not fainted, walked off with some of the women. Suddenly she broke from them, running to the left. Seeing a cross colored like a rainbow, she dropped to her knees.

Our Lady was standing before the cross with tears in her eyes. She repeated several times: "Peace, peace, peace, be reconciled with one another."

The Police Intervene

On the fourth afternoon, the police arrived at Bijakovici and took the six young people to Citluk.

After questioning at the police station, they were sent to a local doctor, Dr. Ante Vujevic. Ivan was in the doctor's office for an hour. Vicka was next but when she had been there for fifteen minutes the children insisted on leaving as six o'clock approached. They took a taxi, except for Ivan who was taken home by relatives and did not come to the hillside that evening.

The crowd was immense and disorganized. The children were separated from each other. A priest from the parish, Father Zrinko Cuvalo and his friend Father Viktor Kosir found themselves near Marija and Jakov. They saw the light and Father Zrinko describes how Marija ran up the hill at immense speed— miraculous speed. Father Viktor Kosir supports this: "Suddenly Marija started getting red in the face, exclaiming, 'Look, look, look!' Jakov did not say anything and they flew away. To me it was an unbelievable speed. Marija was dressed in a white shirt and red skirt so I was able to see her as she raced ahead. There was no way I could follow at that speed." Marija later explained that she only saw Our Lady before her, nothing else.

On that evening, Mirjana spoke to the lady of her concern that people accused them of being drug addicts. "Disregard that," was the reply. Ivanka asked the lady her name. "I am the Blessed Virgin Mary," was the reply.

The communication between the Virgin Mary and the children was so constantly interrupted on this day by the milling crowds. As the local people led the four girls and Jakov home, Our Lady appeared again. Marinko describes what happened: "There were five or six of us with the young people, each holding on to one of them as we were leaving the hill. I remember this very well. At once, all together they pulled themselves away from us, saying: "There she is." Then we made a circle around them like we did before, so that the people would not come too close." Our Lady said to the children: "You are my angels, my dear angels." She promised to come again the next day.

Meanwhile Ivan was at home. Concerned about all that had happened, his parents had asked him not to go to the hill. Although, as Ivan said, "I had pains in my

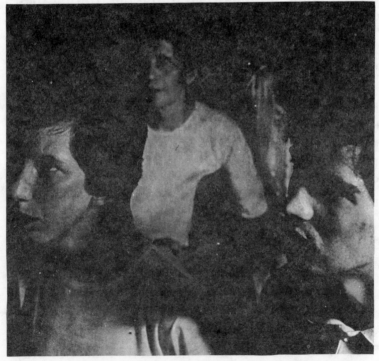

Marija and Ivan during an apparition

stomach" at not going, he obeyed. He stayed around the house, then walked a little way out of the village. Suddenly, Our Lady was in front of him. "She greeted me. She told me to be at peace and to have courage. She left me with a good-bye smile." Seeing Ivan's pain and sadness, his mother promised never again to prevent his going.

On June 29, the local government authorities took the six to the neuropsychiatric department of the local hospital. After thorough testing, the psychiatrist, Doctor Dzudza, pronounced them healthy. They returned home in time to go to the hill. During these evenings Our Lady repeatedly asked that the people "believe as if they see."

On this evening a two and a half year-old boy, Danijel Setka, mute, and unable to walk, was brought to the hill. The children asked the Virgin Mary to cure him. Jakov reported her response: "Let his parents believe that he will be healed." On their way home to Mostar the family stopped at a restaurant. The mute Danijel banged on the table, saying, "I want a drink." Since then his speech has continued to improve and he now walks.

The following afternoon two social workers were sent to take away the four girls and Jakov by car. They were driven around the countryside so that by 6 p.m. they were far from the scene of the apparitions. They called out to the woman who was driving to stop because the lady was coming. She would not stop but was suddenly so blinded by light that she had to pull off the road. The girls and Jakov got out and knelt to pray. Ivanka could see the hillside and all the people. "Everything was in light." The two Communist social workers also saw the light illuminating the hill. "The light was coming towards us," Ivanka continued. In the light was Our Lady; she appeared to them right there on the side of the road.

On this occasion they asked her if she would appear to them in the church. They were being pressured to stop going to the hill. Vicka reports: "They told us: 'You should not make a fool of the people who follow you. Stay by yourselves. People are leaving their jobs; no one wants to do any work. Everyone is following you.' " Vicka also noted that the crowds refused to leave them: "Last night we spoke to the people as much as we could, standing on Marinko's terrace. We repeated everything Our Lady has told us and we could not have been happier. We are always happy but the crowd did not leave us until eleven o'clock. We told them everything but that was not enough."

The apparitions continued daily in the church, rectory or on the hill until August 12 when the police forbade anyone to climb the hill. From then until February 1982 Our Lady appeared first outdoors, then, as winter came, at the home of one or other of the children. Mary prayed and sang hymns with them and continued to teach them.

The Parish Clergy and the Visions

On the second evening, having mistaken the time, Marinko Ivankovic arrived only to meet the children returning down the hill. Ivanka was crying as she ran into her grandmother's arms, to tell her how she had asked Our Lady about her recently dead mother. Seeing the state of things, Marinko decided to go to the priests. "We need someone experienced," he said.

"If this is not genuine, they should not play around with it." He tells how he went to the rectory and asked if there was a priest at home. Father Zrinko was in. He thought to himself: "I would prefer Father Jozo; it would be easier to talk to him." Marinko said to the priest: "Father, I came to tell you. There are some children who say that last night and this evening they saw the Blessed Virgin Mary. They are crying and are troubled. I think that you should come and console them. Talk with them and find out if it is true." Father Zrinko shrugged off the story and refused to go.

Father Zrinko Cuvalo, a Franciscan, had been at St. James for only nine months. He did not know any of the children concerned, nor their families. The children grew to fear him because he rejected them and because of his total disbelief. When anyone tried to speak to him on the subject, he would go out to the garden, as he said, "to do something worthwhile, instead of wasting time."

Nonetheless, he did go on the fourth evening. Father Viktor Kosir says he invited Father Zrinko for a visit on June 29. "Father Zrinko was noticeably different, quiet, but he did not indicate what was on his mind." By the next day Father Viktor had heard the news and went over to Medjugorje, as he said, "to be of some help." He was there when people gave them tape recordings of the events on the hill and the children were interviewed by the clergy for the first time. Father

Zrinko went to the hillside with Father Viktor on the fourth evening.

The parish priest, Father Jozo Zovko, was away at the time attending a seminar at Zagreb. He also had been a short time at Medjugorje—nine months—and did not know any of the six children. People had grown to love and admire him in those months. On June 27, he was in Mostar to visit his mother in the hospital and knew nothing of the events at Medjugorje. Marinko's wife, Dragica tells the story:

> On June 27, I was at work and a metal slab fell on me injuring my hand and breaking my leg. I was taken to the hospital in Mostar and there while I was waiting in front of the hospital Father Jozo came up and asked: "What happened, Dragica?" I shouted at him: "Nothing, nothing! Don't waste time with me! Where have you been? Don't you know Our Lady has appeared?" "Who told you that?" he said. "The children," I replied; "Five, six have seen Our Lady for two evenings. Zrinko hasn't taken it seriously."

Father Jozo Zovko was sceptical. In fact, he left the scene on June 29, when thousands came to the hill. However, seeing the crowds wandering aimlessly on the hill and around the church, he offered them the sacrament of Penance and began an evening Mass. Suddenly, however, people noticed a change in him. He began preaching with fire. This is confirmed by seventy-five young people from Posusje who went to Medjugorje (about eight-five miles) on foot. Father Jozo had been there but they said: "We know Father

Jozo; that isn't like him. It's like Jesus speaking through him." Later, the Bishop of Mostar asked Father Jozo plainly: "Have you seen Our Lady?" He answered, "Yes."

A month earlier, in May 1981, another Franciscan, Father Tomislav Vlasic, had gone to Rome for an international meeting of leaders of the Charismatic Renewal. During the conference he asked some of the leaders to pray with him for the healing of the Church in Yugoslavia. One of those praying, Sister Briege McKenna, had a mental picture of Father Vlasic seated and surrounded by a great crowd; from the seat flowed streams of water. Another, Emile Tardiff OP, said in prophecy, "Do not fear, I am sending you my Mother." A few weeks later Our Lady began appearing in Medjugorje.

Father Tomislav Vlasic first went to Medjugorje on June 29. Then he was transferred there and remained as spiritual director to the six children. In early August, Father Zovko said to him: "Be prepared to take my place."

On August 17, agents of the secret police and the military surrounded the church and the rectory. They raided the house, taking away documents, letters, books and money. The sisters' convent was entered and policewomen stripped the sisters to their underclothing. The convent itself was sequestered and subsequently gutted. Father Zovko was arrested, charged with sedition and imprisoned for three and a half years.

Two other Franciscans are in jail: Fathers Ferdo Vlasic and Jozo Krizic, for eight and five and a half years respectively, though the former is sixty-two years old. One is the editor and the other the secretary of a Franciscan magazine *Nasa Ognijista* ("Home Fires") published chiefly to keep Croatian emigrants in touch with home. It was an article about the apparitions which led to their arrest.

Pope John Paul II is said to have questioned the Yugoslavian ambassador about the imprisonment of these men. The ambassador acknowledged it was a mistake and the sentences were halved. Father Zovko has recently been released although the other two remain in prison. But they are joyful. Father Zovko says: "Every good priest should see the inside of a prison and suffer for the faith. I have seen the living dead here and I have also discovered in prison what the Catholic faith is and the strength and dignity of life it offers."

Father Zrinko has come to believe in the apparitions. He took over the parish and stood by the young people and the parishioners through all these difficulties until finally exhausted he was transferred.

III

Mary's Appearances Continue

By Lucy Rooney SND

Medjugorje Today

The white church stands alone on a green. To the right are the remains of the sisters' convent. The people built the church themselves between 1937 and 1969. At the time they wondered why they were making it so big. Nearby is the house of the three Franciscan priests, with its outside staircase leading to the living quarters above. At ground level is the parish wine press and the huge barrels where the wine ferments for five years. The other long room here, damp and smelling like Bacchus, is where the grapes are piled in troughs. Normally this damp place is the catechetical centre, for as Catholic schools are not allowed, religion is taught at the church. When the Franciscans sought building permission for a place more suitable for the children, they were told they had all they needed. Yet upstairs, the three, sometimes four sisters sleep in one room while the priests make do

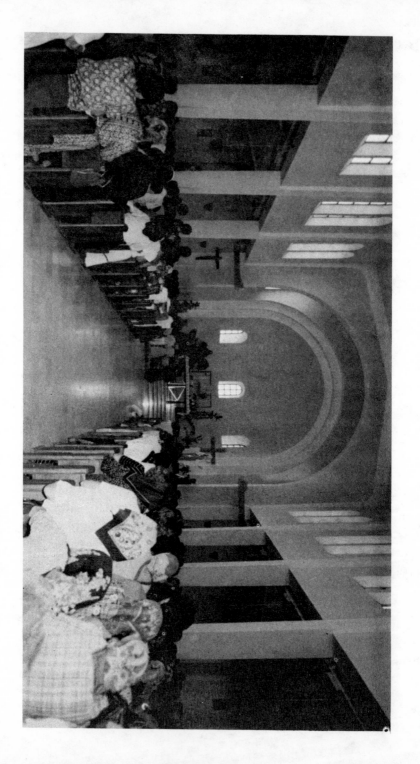

The interior of the parish church of St. James in Medjugorje

with beds in the office, dining room and the small library. Nor can they build for the pilgrims. A spring running into a trough is the only facility for thousands and there is no shelter in the open plain from the relentless sun or deluging rain.

Since mid-February 1982 the six young people come to the church for their nightly visions. During the school term Mirjana has not been present but the Blessed Virgin appeared to her until recently at Sarajevo.

Each evening there is a service of reconciliation at the church while outside as many priests as can be mustered (up to thirty) hear confessions, the people kneeling on the grass. On first Fridays, these priests hear each others' confessions. So effective is the sacrament in the new rite that physical healings have followed good confessions. Before Mass, those of the six young people who are at Medjugorje lead the rosary. At the end of the rosary they go into a room off the sanctuary; only the few people admitted to this room see the children as they speak to Our Lady. An eye witness writes:

We three visitors were in one of the sacristies off the sanctuary. As the rosary finished, the four children who were there during our stay came into the room. They went to a table against the wall and looked at the objects left there for Mary to bless. They recalled the things they had been asked to say to her; then, facing the table and about four feet from the wall, they began to pray the Our Father, Hail Mary and Glory Be . . . Suddenly, with an exclamation, they fell to their knees in one concerted movement, their eyes fixed on a spot above them, their lips moving soundlessly, their faces expressing delight, absorption. Their gaze did not flicker even when photo flashes went off with the camera held close.

After a few minutes they seemed to reach forward with exclamations—obviously Mary was leaving them; they resumed vocal prayer, stood up and moved to one side.

The Mass began then and we followed it from the sacristy with the children. After Mass they went out into the sanctuary, leading the people in prayer for healing. Usually Mary tells them to say the Our Father, the Hail Mary and Glory Be seven times. . . . Father Vlasic then offers a prayer for every kind of healing. The people leave quietly after this, except for any who want individual prayer. These come up to the sanctuary where the young people and Father Vlasic pray with them.

Mary has told them, "I cannot heal; only God can. I need your prayers and sacrifices to help me." There have been physical healings at Medjugorje but the greatest graces have been conversions and growth in prayer and faith.

Thousands of pilgrims come to Medjugorje. Local coach firms have been forbidden by the government to take people there, so, as few have cars, they come miles on foot. Coaches arrive from other republics of Yugoslavia and from Italy, Austria and Germany. British, American and other nationalities come in increasing numbers. There is nothing spectacular to be seen now that the children do not see Mary in the presence of the crowd, yet all who come go away greatly moved and graced.

Medjugorje is very much a young people's place. On the feast of the Exaltation of the Cross in 1983 (celebrated on the Sunday), about 100,000 came, over half of them young people. Transport being forbidden, they came mostly bare-footed, walking to the isolated village and climbing up the rocky mountain to the great cross on the ridge—a cross put there in 1933 to commemorate the nineteen hundredth year of our redemption. Older people say: "The young fast and pray more than we do." Yet before the coming of Mary, half the young people hardly knew how to say the rosary. Four days after the first apparition, Ivan's mother said: "Yesterday, for the first time since he was born, I found a rosary in the pocket of his trousers." The parish of Medjugorje is transformed. Their priests told us that the people have learned forgiveness; there are no quarrels any more, old people are not left alone, hospitality is given freely and all work together clearing land and building houses. They form one community with their priests. This naturally explosive people remained calm even during the raids and arrests of 1981.

The Message

What is the meaning of these events? What is the reason for the unprecedented length of time the reported apparitions of the Mother of God have continued?

It seems that for the six girls and boys concerned, there are three reasons. First they are being formed and taught individually. Father Tomislav Vlasic said in 1982 that he had the impression that the teachings were following the pattern of the liturgical year. Then late that year the Blessed Virgin began recounting her own life to Jakov and the girls. This has not been so with Ivan. He was asked: "How do you spend your time with Our Lady since she does not speak to you about her life as she does to the others?" Ivan replied: "We pray together."

All six say that they pray and sing hymns with Mary. They ask her questions. Sometimes she says: "That is enough questions." She advises, encourages and corrects them. Although the children say that they speak in normal voices, bystanders cannot hear what is said and see only the slightest lip movements. The six can hear each other except when Mary has a message or a correction for an individual. Sometimes one has tears in his or her eyes, and then the others know what is happening.

The second reason is that they have been called to live and transmit a message. The core of the message was given on the third evening when, instructed by Marinko, they asked the Lady, "Why have you come?" She replied: "I want to be with you; to convert and to reconcile everyone." Even on the second day, Marija's vision of Our Lady at the foot of the cross showed the Mother of God in tears, saying: "Peace, peace, peace. Be reconciled with each other." When asked if she had another name, her response was: "The Queen of Peace."

Statue of Our Lady in the church at Medjugorje

The message of Medjugorje is peace: peace through conversion. The way to conversion is fourfold: faith, daily prayer, monthly confession, fasting.

One evening in early August 1981, the word *MIR* (Croatian for "peace") was seen written in light above the hill where the cross stands. Father Jozo and the villagers are witnesses to this. Mary has asked for June 25 to be kept as the feast of Our Lady Queen of Peace. When the children said to her: "The twenty-fourth" (the first day of her appearing), she said: "But you ran away that day."

Our Lady spoke urgently of the need for conversion: "Do not delay . . . The only word I wish to say is "conversion." To the whole world. I am saying this to you to tell everybody. I ask only for conversion. Be ready for everything and be converted. Give up everything that goes against conversion." (April 26, 1983).

From the beginning, Our Lady called for faith. "Let them believe as if they see"; "believe firmly." "There are many believers who do not pray; faith cannot be alive without prayer." When the children asked at the request of a priest if people should pray to Jesus or to Mary, her answer was: "Please pray to Jesus. I am his Mother and I intercede for you with him. But all prayer goes to Jesus. I will help, I will pray, but everything does not depend only on me. It depends also on your strength, the strength of those who pray." She went on: "As for petitions, come to me, I know the will of God better than you do." "The Mass is the greatest prayer. You must be prepared and be perfect and humble at Mass." On one occasion Mary urged the children: "Pray, pray for them (sinners). Pray now, today. I need your prayer and penance."

Speaking to the children about the sacrament of Reconciliation she described it as "a medicine for the Church of the West." She said: "Whole regions of the Church would be healed if believers would go to confession once a month."

A theologian, Father Celestin Tomic of Zagreb, who had never been to Medjugorje, nonetheless believed in the truth of the apparitions because of the confessions that he heard of people who had been changed there.

All the families of the parish now fast each Friday on bread and water as Our Lady asked. The six young people, the priests and sisters also fast on Wednesday. When the six began fasting for nine days in preparation for each of the major feasts, the priests and sisters joined them. One of the latter observed: "We might cheat in taking a cup of coffee but the children never do." It seems that Our Lady has not thought this fasting excessive, so urgent is her concern over the catastrophe threatening the world: "Christians have forgotten that they can stop war and even natural calamities by prayer and fasting." No one is exempt from fasting, she said, except the seriously ill. Prayer and almsgiving cannot substitute for fasting.

A third reason for the reported apparitions at Medjugorje is an important ecumenical one. Yugoslavia is bordered to the east by Soviet bloc countries: Hungary, Rumania, Bulgaria. To the west is free Europe. It is thus an ideological frontier. The villages which make up the parish of Medjugorje are grouped at the corner of a triangle of Muslim, Orthodox and Catholic areas. On the whole Croats are Catholic, Serbians are Orthodox and the Slavs who are descendants of converts to Islam during the Turkish occupation, are Moslem. Religion and nationalism are so identified that religion becomes divisive. Part of the civil authorities' fear of events at Medjugorje was that it might be a plot to further Croatian nationalism. The place chosen by Mary is therefore a religious frontier. On this subject, the children say that Our Lady told them: "In God there are no divisions and there are no religions. You in the world have made the divisions. The one mediator is Jesus Christ. Which religion you belong to cannot be a matter of indifference. The presence of the Spirit is not the same in every church."

Mirjana says that the Blessed Virgin "pointed out that religious people, especially those in the villages, for example here in Medjugorje, separate themselves too much from persons of the Serbian and Moslem faiths. That is not good. She has always stated that there is only one God and that people have divided themselves. You are not a Christian if you do not respect others, Moslems and Serbians."

The Secrets and the Signs

Part of this message of impending catastrophe and the means for mitigating it, consists of ten secrets. Mirjana received all ten and then her visions of Our Lady ceased. The others have received varying numbers. They say that the secrets are about the world, the

Exterior view of the Medjugorje parish church

parish and local Church, and the whole Church. They will be told when to reveal them. The six, who are not remarkably intelligent, are yet adroit in countering questions which come too near the secrets. When pressed by a Church official who said: "You could write down the secrets, put them in an envelope, seal them and leave them with me," Jakov (then aged ten) replied: "I could write down the secrets, put them in an envelope and leave them at home."

One of these secrets concerns a great sign which Our Lady will leave at the place of her first appearance. The children know what the sign will be and at least four of them know the date. It will be a permanent, visible sign. Of it Our Lady said: "Hasten your conversion. Do not wait for the sign that has been announced. For unbelievers it will be too late to be converted. For you who believe this is an opportunity to be converted and to deepen your faith."

Our Lady says that this permanent, visible sign is to convert, if possible, even unbelievers. Many miraculous healings will come with it. She said to the children: "I know many will not believe you and many enthused for the faith will grow cold. You should stay steadfast and urge the people to steadfast prayer, penance and conversion. In the end you will be the happiest." The Virgin Mary said that she has prayed for this permanent, visible sign and said to the children: "You do not need a sign, you must be a sign." She told them that they are like water pipes; if they get rusted, the water cannot pass freely.

There have been signs visible to all at Medjugorje.

On August 2, 1981, late in the afternoon, one hundred and fifty pople saw the sun spinning towards them. They cried out, prayed, ran away. Their experiences differed: some saw angels with trumpets coming out of the sun; others saw Our Lady; others, the Sacred Heart of Jesus. All saw a white cloud upon the hill and the sun returning to its normal place. The episode lasted fifteen minutes.

On another occasion a fire blazed up between earth and heaven on the hillside. When the police rushed up, they found nothing, and no sign of burning. All saw the word *MIR* ("peace") written across the sky in letters of light. In August 1982, Ivan, who was home for the holidays, was on the hillside with some friends. Our Lady appeared to him and said: "Now I will give you a sign to strengthen your faith." Two bright beams of light were then seen coming down, one on the church and one on the cross on the hill. One of the boys with Ivan said: "I'll never sin again."

The cross erected on the hill in 1933 has been the scene of a number of signs. Often it has been seen as a pillar of light, or as the tau sign. On October 22, 1981, for half an hour, many saw the cross turned to a pillar of light with the figure of a woman, as a statue, at its foot. Her hands were extended and she was looking towards the parish church. Some of the witnesses used binoculars. The pilgrims at the church were kneeling, praying, singing and uttering cries of joy, their faces bright with exultation. Mary stated: "All these signs are to reinforce your faith until I send a permanent, visible sign."

What do the young people see?

It is difficult to speak of "the young people" collectively as they vary in age (in 1983) from twelve to nineteen.

The eldest is Vicka, curly haired, vivacious, forceful. Recently, Our Lady said that not all the older children should leave Medjugorje each day for secondary school at Mostar; one should stay with Jakov. Vicka volunteered and now works in the tobacco fields. Jakov is blond and small for his age. He is never still except in the presence of Our Lady. He is probably the most intelligent of the six. The others say he is the strongest. Ivanka is more regularly good-looking, and at surface level, more superficial. She obviously enjoys the things that interest young people. Ivan joined the Franciscan minor seminary but recently returned home. He still wants to be a priest. He and all the children except Jakov and Mirjana have difficulty with their studies. Marija is quiet, retiring. All describe her as a "beautiful" character. She has a kind word for everyone she meets and has been called by Our Lady to "much, much prayer." The six say that the Blessed Virgin told them she would be happy if they entered the religious life, but that she leaves them entirely free. Ivanka says: "She said to us it is her wish for us to go to the convent, but only those who want to; we should not go and disgrace the faith and the Church." Mirjana has chosen to continue her studies. She is perhaps the most mature of the six.

All these normal young girls and boys fast drastically and have spent hours in church every evening over the last three years. They deal courteously with crowds, interrogations, photographers, adulation, disbelief, opprobrium, threats from the Communist authorities and police.

The center and source is what they see each evening: Mary, a creature, yet Mother of God. Usually, they say, Mary is smiling and praising God with her arms raised. When asked what Our Lady looks like, they replied that she is "clothed in holiness." Light always precedes her coming. She stands on a cloud which grows wider the longer she stays. Her mantle is white and the long dress without cincture is a translucent grey. Sometimes Mary has appeared with the child Jesus in her arms. On great feasts she is more glorious than ever. On the feast of the Assumption she was dressed in gold. An interpreter, Sister Janja, who learned English in the USA translated the children's comment as: "Boy! Was she beautiful!" When asked if they look forward to each evening, their exclamations needed no interpretation. Because of Mary's increased glory on her feast days, they looked forward especially to seeing her on December 8 (1981), the feast of her Immaculate Conception. But when Mary appeared she was very serious. She fell to her knees and prayed: "My beloved Son, forgive the world for so many sins."

Four of the young people have been shown hell and Mary said: "This is the punishment for those who do not love God; many are going there." They also saw purgatory and Mary told them: "These people are waiting for your prayers and sacrifices." All six have seen heaven. On one occasion Mary said she would take two of the children to heaven for a while. Jakov and Vicka then simply disappeared and were away twenty minutes. Jakov's mother was one of the witnesses to this.

The Virgin Mary comes over delightfully in these encounters. When the children asked her: "How long are you going to appear to us?" She replied, "Why, am I already boring you?"

At the time of writing, late 1983, Our Lady seems to be teaching each of the young people different things. Vicka, for example, is learning about Our Lady's life. Our Lady is telling Ivanka about future world events. She continues to encourage all of them to recommend that everyone pray and fast. She especially recommends prayer for Church authorities and that God will pour his Holy Spirit on the world.

Conclusion

Father Tomislav Vlasic, the director of the six young people, is the usual preacher at the evening Mass at St. James, Medjugorje. Father Vlasic is determined that Medjugorje should not be used by Croatian nationalists or any group to further their political ends. His sermons are entirely gospel-centered. He says: "The good news speaks for itself; just present it. The gospel loses its force if it becomes political." He is opposed to the commercialization of Medjugorje and to its political use. It is a place of silence and prayer where people come for conversion more than for physical healing. There are many physical healings, but the Virgin Mary, Mother of God, putting all things in perspective said: "I cannot heal you. Only God can heal. Pray; I will be with you. Believe firmly, fast, do penance. I will help you as much as is within my power. God is helping everybody. I am not God. I need your prayers and sacrifices to help me."

When asked "What is the reason for Our Lady's apparitions?" Ivanka answered: "I think the world is going in the wrong direction and she has come to reconcile the world." Her questioners continued: "What would you say to those who are against Our

Ivan, Marija, Ivanka and Father Tomislav

Lady?" Ivanka replied: "I would tell them: Let everyone be converted. There is a God. That's it."

The Church has not yet announced that the apparitions at Medjugorje are worthy of faith and the events remain under investigation. But (a) the best trained actors would have difficulty playing such a part, let alone these ordinary youngsters; (b) the doctrine is sound and is beyond the capacity of the six children; (c) the devil would not want our conversion, faith, prayer and fasting, so the possibility of diabolic deception can be ruled out; and (d) the fruits of the apparitions—in the lives of the young people and in the parish—are so positive as to be the best reason for believing the apparitions to be authentic.

IV

Interview with Mirjana

The following interview took place in the village of Medjugorje on January 10, 1983. Father Tomislav Vlasic OFM asked Mirjana to speak into a tape recorder microphone so as to have a permanent record of some of her experiences. Here is a translation from the Croatian of their recorded conversation.

TOMISLAV:
Mirjana, we have not seen each other for some time and I would like to ask you to tell me something about the apparitions of the Blessed Virgin Mary, especially the events connected with you, with your experiences of the Blessed Virgin Mary.

MIRJANA:
I have been with the Blessed Virgin Mary now for eighteen months already and I have become very close to her. I feel she loves me with a motherly love. I am able to ask her anything I want. I ask her about heaven, hell and purgatory and to explain some things that were not clear to me. For example, I asked her how

God could be so unmerciful as to throw people into hell to suffer forever. I thought, if a person makes a mistake then he goes to prison, he stays there for a while and he is forgiven . . . but in hell for ever? Then she told me that those people who go to hell do not like God. There, they curse him even more than before. They become a part of that hell and they do not think about their deliverance. She told me that in purgatory there are levels: the lowest level for those that are closest to hell, and then higher and higher towards heaven.

TOMISLAV:
Did Our Lady talk to you about whether many people today go to hell?

MIRJANA:
I asked her about that not long ago and she said today most of them go to purgatory.

TOMISLAV:
That means that not many go directly to heaven.

MIRJANA:
Yes, not many.

TOMISLAV:
Did you ask what are the conditions for a person to enter heaven?

MIRJANA:
I did not ask the conditions but probably we could

presuppose those. God is not looking for some great believers, but simply that you respect your faith and live your life peacefully, without any malice, meanness or lying.

TOMISLAV:
Are you interpreting that as you understand it?

MIRJANA:
Yes. After I had talked to her I came to that conclusion. Miracles do not have to be done, or some great penance. Just a simple, peaceful life.

TOMISLAV:
Did you see hell?

MIRJANA:
No, I didn't want to.

TOMISLAV:
You didn't want to see it?

MIRJANA:
No.

TOMISLAV:
Purgatory?

MIRJANA:
Purgatory neither. Just heaven. She described purgatory to me as I said—with the levels.

TOMISLAV:
Well, besides heaven, hell and purgatory, what else has
Our Lady said to you recently?

MIRJANA:
She told me to say that many people in our time look at
the faith through priests. If the priest isn't good then it
means there is no God. She said: "You don't go to
church to see the priest, to look into his private life, you
go to church to pray and to hear the word of God
through the priest." That has to be explained to people
because many are turning away from the faith, most of
them because of priests.

Another thing: as you know, she told me the tenth
secret and also the ninth. She also told me something
that was very important and very soul-stirring.

It's like this. Sometime ago, it's as if God and the
devil talked and the devil said that people believe in
God only while things go well for them. But when they
go badly they stop believing in him. Then people
blame God or say he doesn't exist.

Then God allowed the devil to take one century to
rule the world and he chose the twentieth century. The
time has come. We can see that, because rarely does
one person stand by another. People have become
mixed up and nobody can live with anybody. There are
divorces, children who lose their lives. Concretely she
meant in all this the interference of the devil. The devil
has also entered a convent. Two nuns called me from
that convent. He entered one of the sisters there and
she didn't know what to do. She was just jerking and
screaming and trying to injure herself. Then Our Lady

said that the devil had entered her. She explained all that to me and said that blessed water should be sprinkled on her, that she should be taken to church to be prayed over, that she herself should pray when she is normal. Then the devil left her, but he entered two other sisters. And you know, Father, Sister Marinka from Sarajevo has heard him screaming outside when she went to bed. She was smart. She immediately crossed herself and started praying. That could happen to anybody in our time. One should not be afraid, because if you get afraid it means that you are not firm, that you do not know God. All you need do is trust God and start praying.

TOMISLAV:
You mentioned that the devil has entered marriages.

MIRJANA:
That is just the beginning of his rule.

TOMISLAV:
You mean: was.

MIRJANA:
Yes, that was the beginning.

TOMISLAV:
When?

MIRJANA:
She started to talk to me about that when the sister called me. That was fifteen days ago. It is as if he

started to rule around two years ago. Before it was quite small but now it is terrible. You know for yourself. Hardly anybody can stand anyone else. Maybe you don't know because you are separated from the people. But when you live in the village—everybody has something against someone else and something to say against them.

TOMISLAV:

That behavior of people against each other, that is through the influence of the devil. The devil does not have to be in them for them to behave that way.

MIRJANA:

No. No, the devil is not in them but they are under the influence of the devil. He also enters into some divorced couples.

Our Lady said to prevent that at least to some extent there is a need for communal prayer, family prayer. She emphasized family prayer the most. We need to have at least one sacred thing in the house and the house should be blessed regularly.

She has also pointed out many times that religious people especially those in the village, for example here in Medjugorje, keep away from Serbians and Moslems. Often people make fun of them. That is not good. She has always pointed out that there is only one God and that people have separated themselves. You cannot believe, you are not a Christian, if you don't respect other religions, Moslem and Serbian.

TOMISLAV:
Let me ask you a question: What is the role of Jesus Christ if the Moslem religion is acceptable?

MIRJANA:
I didn't talk about that with her. She just explained what I said. She said: "Especially in villages." This disunity of religions . . . everybody's religion should be respected, guarding your own for yourself and for your children.

TOMISLAV:
Tell me this: How is the devil especially active today? Did she tell you through whom and in what he manifests himself the most?

MIRJANA:
Most of all through people who do not have a balanced character, who are divided in themselves, torn in different directions. But he also enters the lives of great believers. You saw those sisters. After all, they are believers, but despite this he entered among them. He would rather convert real believers than unbelievers. How can I explain that? You saw what happened to me. His goal is to bring as many believers as possible to himself.

TOMISLAV:
What do you mean, "what happened to me"? Is that what you mentioned before?

MIRJANA:
Yes, when I talked about it.

TOMISLAV:
You have never described what happened into a tape recorder. Please try to describe it.

MIRJANA:
It was about six months ago. I don't know exactly. As usual I locked myself in my room. I was alone, waiting for Our Lady. I just knelt, without yet making the sign of the cross. Suddenly there was a flash of light and the devil appeared. It was as if something told me that this was a devil. I looked at him in great surprise, naturally. I was expecting Our Lady and something like that appeared to me.

He looked horrible. He was all kind of black and had . . . something horrifying, full of some dreadfulness. I stared. I didn't understand what he wanted. I started to faint and then I passed out completely. When I came to, I saw him still standing there and he was laughing. It was as if he gave me some strength to accept him normally. He started explaining that I was going to be more beautiful and happier than other people—things like that. The only thing I didn't need was Our Lady. And I didn't need faith. "Our Lady has brought you only sufferings and difficulties." He would bring me the most beautiful things. Something in me—I don't know what it was, whether it was in me or something in my soul—told me: No! No! No! I started shaking. There was real torment inside me and he disappeared. Then Our Lady appeared and when she came she gave me back my strength, helped me to understand him; that is the way it is. She told me: "This is a bad time, but it will end."

TOMISLAV:
Did Our Lady say anything else then?

MIRJANA:
She didn't say anything. She told me it was going to happen like that and that she would talk about it later.

TOMISLAV:
You said the twentieth century was left to the devil.

MIRJANA:
Yes.

TOMISLAV:
Is that the century looked at chronologically until the year 2000 or more generally speaking?

MIRJANA:
No, I meant that generally. She also told me and explained my secrets. I put them all with code letters, all the dates, so that I would not forget, or in case anything happened by accident.

If for example the day after tomorrow one secret is to be fulfilled I have a right to choose a priest, any priest I want, two or three days in advance and tell him: "The day after tomorrow this is going to happen." Then he can do whatever he chooses with this information. He can write it down and read it out after it happens to show that it was known. Or he can tell people about it; for example: "Tomorrow this is what is going to happen." It is up to him to decide what to do.

TOMISLAV:
Have the secrets you received been told to anybody else, to the generations before, maybe to other visionaries?

MIRJANA:
I can't answer that, because you know all the secrets that have been given in the past—or maybe not all, but you do know some of them.

TOMISLAV:
I don't know them all, but if you can't talk then we won't talk about it. That's fine. Do you know when the secrets are going to start being revealed?

MIRJANA:
Yes, I know the date of every secret.

TOMISLAV:
You can't say anything about it?

MIRJANA:
No.

TOMISLAV:
Let us speak generally then. Somebody here was saying that three secrets are going to be revealed before the great sign and then after the great sign the others

are going to be revealed one by one. Is this correct or not?

MIRJANA:
It isn't like that. First of all some secrets are going to be revealed, not too many, and people will realize that Our Lady was here. They will understand the sign. When Jakov said that the mayor would be the first to run to the hill, he meant in general, people of the higher class.

They will understand the sign as a place where they can be converted. They will go to the hill and pray and they will be forgiven. When I asked her about some unbelievers, she told me: "You should pray for them and they themselves should pray!" But when I asked recently, she told me: "Let them be converted while there is time." She didn't say that they should be prayed for.

TOMISLAV:
Then nothing specific can be said until the moment when Our Lady lets you say it?

MIRJANA:
Yes.

TOMISLAV:
Can we say that some of your secrets are of a personal nature?

MIRJANA:
No. I don't have any secret that is for me personally.

TOMISLAV:
You don't? But Ivan has his personal secrets.

MIRJANA:
With me they are like this: for mankind generally, for
the world, for Medjugorje, for some other areas and
information about the sign.

TOMISLAV:
Well, about the sign—that is for this parish.

MIRJANA:
Yes, for Medjugorje, but there is something else.

TOMISLAV:
Yes?

MIRJANA:
Nothing for me personally.

TOMISLAV:
You have received the last secret?

MIRJANA:
Yes, I have; the tenth.

TOMISLAV:
Can you say what it relates to?

MIRJANA:
No. I can say that the eighth was worse than the other
seven. For a long time I prayed for it to be mitigated;

every time she came, I pestered her for it to be mitigated. Then she told me that people should pray for this. So in Sarajevo I asked many believers to pray for it. One day she told me that she had succeeded in mitigating the secret.

Then the ninth and tenth secret came and it was even worse and the tenth was altogether bad and it can't be mitigated at all. I can't say what it is about because if I said something I would give everything away.

TOMISLAV:
You don't have to say. Anyway, this means that the tenth secret is as you say and it is going to happen?

MIRJANA:
Yes.

TOMISLAV:
Unavoidably?

MIRJANA:
Yes, it is going to happen.

TOMISLAV:
What does Our Lady say? The secret can't be averted, but can we prepare ourselves?

MIRJANA:
Yes, prepare! She said that people should prepare themselves spiritually, they should be ready and should not panic and they should be reconciled in their

souls. I mean they should be ready for it. They should be ready to die tomorrow; they should accept God so that they are not afraid since they have God in them and they can accept everything. I know nobody can accept death easily, but still they should be at peace in their souls, knowing that they are believers, that they are with God and that they will be accepted by him.

TOMISLAV:
It means a complete conversion and surrender to God is needed?

MIRJANA:
Yes.

TOMISLAV:
Now after these ten secrets, after these eighteen months of apparitions, what would you tell people to do? What would you say to priests? What would you say to the Pope and to the bishops without revealing the secrets, about all that Our Lady wishes to be done?

MIRJANA:
First of all I would like to tell them how it was for me at the end. . . .

TOMISLAV:
That's fine.

MIRJANA:
Two days before Christmas 1982, she said to me she would be with me for the last time at Christmas. But I

didn't believe it. I thought, "It won't be like that." On Christmas Day she was with me for forty-five minutes and we talked about many things. We really put everything together. I made requests for many people and then she gave me a very dear gift. She said she would appear to me each birthday while I am alive, independently of the sign or anything else. And she will appear to me when something difficult happens to me; something very difficult, not some small everyday thing but something that will hurt me badly. She will come to help me.

But now I have to face life without her and without her help. I would tell people to convert just as she did: "Be converted while there is time." Do not leave God and your faith. Leave everything, but not that! I would ask priests to help people, because priests turn some people away from the faith. When you become a priest, be a real priest and bring people to the Church. The main thing is that people should be converted and should pray.

TOMISLAV:
Tell me where the main danger comes from?

MIRJANA:
It comes most from godlessness. Nobody believes, or hardly anybody. She actually said to me that faith in Germany, Switzerland and Austria is very bad. Many people there look at their priests and if they are not good then they aren't either. Then they think that there is no God and no faith.

There is one priest in B. to whom a rich man left

money to build a home for old people; but he built a hotel. Now people in that city have completely turned away from the faith. How could a priest ignore a man's last wish and build a hotel for himself instead to make money? People should understand that they do not have to look at him and his private life but at what he says, just what he says through God: God's word.

TOMISLAV:
Our Lady introduced herself as Queen of Peace. Why?

MIRJANA:
Can't you see for yourself that the situation in the world is horrible? Wars everywhere; the situation is tense. Peace is needed, just peace—peace in the soul first, then it will be ...

TOMISLAV:
So it could be said that the message of Our Lady is a message of peace?

MIRJANA:
Yes. The main thing is peace of soul. If you have peace in your soul, then you have it around you.

TOMISLAV:
It comes as a consequence of faith in God and surrender to him.

MIRJANA:
Yes, as a consequence of prayer, penance and fasting.

TOMISLAV:
Our Lady sees that peace in the world could be brought about like that. But some things are going to happen anyway. Why?

MIRJANA:
They have to happen. The world has become very bad today. It cares very little about the faith. She was telling me the bad level faith has reached. For example, I live in Sarajevo now and if I put a simple cross around my neck and walk along the street, how many people would say, "Look at that sensible girl!" But how many others would say, "How stupid she is!" meaning that she is out of date and all sorts of bad things. There are very few who would say, "She is a sensible girl!" That's it.

And they curse God, Jesus, his Mother, his Father, at every step. They do very bad things; evil is being done everywhere. It makes sense that God cannot accept it any more.

TOMISLAV:
Why do you think Our Lady is always repeating: prayer and penance?

MIRJANA:
If you pray to God, as you said last night in your homily, then you receive that peace in your soul, that tranquility. You open your heart to God. If you have God in your heart and in your soul, then you will never cause evil to anybody; you will not curse, you will do nothing bad, you will be good. You will be a believer

and you will do good if you have God, if you pray, if you open your heart to God.

TOMISLAV:
But Our Lady says: "Pray for others."

MIRJANA:
I always pray for unbelievers, because maybe they don't understand how they are failing in their lives. They don't understand how much they will suffer later because of this. I pray to God that he will convert them and give them some sign, that he will open their souls a little so that they can accept the faith.

TOMISLAV:
I understand that with prayer we open ourselves to God but Our Lady is always stressing prayer for others; prayer and fasting. Do you feel that with prayer and fasting we can bring a balance into the world? Do you feel that reparation is needed for so many sins; that those sins can be made up for with prayer and fasting so to speak?

MIRJANA:
Yes. A great deal can be done with prayer and fasting. She herself said that wars could be stopped and catastrophes prevented with prayer. With prayer and fasting! Naturally prayer is needed if you see a fellow man who doesn't accept God.

You have to pray for him to open his heart. For example, in Sarajevo I talk with unbelievers a lot. I

explain some things to them so that they can understand at least a little. Sometimes it is not their fault, for
example if religion was not given to them in their
childhood, or later if they abandoned it. I pray to God
to open their hearts so that they accept him.

TOMISLAV:
How do you succeed when you talk to people about
that? How do they receive you? Do they accept you?

MIRJANA:
It's like this. First of all it begins, for instance, in the
classroom. They don't know that Our Lady has appeared to me, but they know that I believe. When
somebody curses God I ask them not to do that or at
least not in front of me. Then they ask me if I believe. I
tell them that I do. So that way we start to talk. Then I
try to explain some things to them. I try to explain
about God, who he is, what he wants. Then they begin
to understand me. Many of them have asked me to
write a prayer for them, so that they can read it in the
evening. And they really accept a lot. Just last night I
converted a man. When you convert somebody, when
you introduce somebody to the faith, you feel that you
have done something great. A feeling of great peace
comes into my soul, a special joy if I explain the faith to
somebody or help him find a way to God. Somehow my
whole soul starts glittering.

TOMISLAV:
Was there any message for priests, or bishops?

MIRJANA:
No. A long time ago she said that they should accept us, help us as much as they can, pray more, and do penance.

TOMISLAV:
Them too?

MIRJANA:
Yes.

TOMISLAV:
But there were no special messages for any priest?

MIRJANA:
Not exactly.

TOMISLAV:
For the Pope?

MIRJANA:
No. I never asked anything for the Pope.

TOMISLAV:
You didn't ask.

MIRJANA:
No.

TOMISLAV:
And she didn't say anything herself?

MIRJANA:
No.

TOMISLAV:
Can you tell me something from the conversation you had with her?

MIRJANA:
I don't know what to say. Maybe about when she stopped appearing to me?

TOMISLAV:
Yes.

MIRJANA:
I asked her why it was like that, and why I had to be the first. She said that she had stayed quite a long time, longer than she needed to, but that as this is the last apparition on earth . . .

TOMISLAV:
What do you mean "the last apparition on earth"?

MIRJANA:
It is the last time Jesus or Mary will come to earth.

TOMISLAV:
Appearing?

MIRJANA:
The last time they are appearing exactly like this, so that you can speak with them.

TOMISLAV:

Is this the last apparition in this era, in this period of the Church, or will they never come to earth again?

MIRJANA:

I don't know that. She said this is the last apparition on earth. I don't understand any more than that.

TOMISLAV:

I once asked the other visionaries if this was the last apparition in this period of the history of the Church or if it is something like the end of the world and she will never appear again.

They told me that she had said "in this period."

MIRJANA:

I don't know. She said she will not appear on earth. I don't know if that means in this age. I didn't know I should ask about that.

TOMISLAV:

Did you ever ask about other apparitions in the world—Our Lady's apparitions in our era in other places?

MIRJANA:

She said there was a man in Germany who was always saying: "Be converted while you have time!" He would get on the buses and trains and make people panic. She said there were lots of false prophets in the world in our age and many people who lie and say that they have seen her or Jesus. This is a great sin and we should pray for these people a lot. She and I prayed for two weeks simply for those who are false prophets. They can't see how serious a sin it is to lie about seeing somebody from heaven.

Now, to come back to what we were discussing. I asked her why she had to stop appearing to me. She explained that she had stayed a long time, that having decided to continue with my schooling I have to face life without her help or advice. I have to understand that I am like any other young person—like other girls; that I have to live my life without her and that she will come to me on each birthday. Before this I can think about the questions I should like to ask and what I wish from her.

TOMISLAV:
Among other things you mentioned here that she said: "You have decided to continue at school." If you had decided on a life in a convent do you think she would have continued appearing?

MIRJANA:
I think so. No, I'm not sure. No, I think maybe not! She did say that she had stayed too long, so that means she wouldn't have continued. She didn't intend to stay this long. No, I think she wouldn't have. It would be the same—her gift for each birthday. That is something great, marvelous. She will come for every birthday.

TOMISLAV:
Now, before we leave, is there anything else you would like to say?

MIRJANA:
She told me some things which are for me personally.
She gave me some advice. She said: "Go in God's
peace!"

TOMISLAV:
Did she talk to you about other visionaries and further
apparitions?

MIRJANA:
She told me that, because I am—how can I put it?—
more mature than they are, I should help them a lot; I
must stay with them and talk to them. It is going to be
easier for me than for them. We should understand
each other, stay together—united and not separate
from each other.

TOMISLAV:
She didn't talk about any further development of apparitions to the individuals and to the group?

MIRJANA:
I think it will be like this. When each one learns the
tenth secret then she will stop appearing to him or her.

TOMISLAV:
Mirjana, tell me how you felt after the last meeting with
Our Lady. Was that a difficult parting? What were you
experiencing in your soul? Try to tell me sincerely
what was happening inside you.

MIRJANA:
When she left, I sat like this. I don't know . . . somehow I felt very strange. I thought: this isn't true; she'll come again. I'll pray again at that time and she'll come. I was very restless.

I wanted to be left alone, to stay alone. I locked myself in my room and various thoughts came to me: She will come again; she will not come. I was in real distress. What am I going to do? How am I going to get along without her? Then I would pray for a long time; it was as if I were in a sort of trance. Then when I came to myself I wondered what the reason was for all this; she was not there and would not come again. It was terrible, terrible.

TOMISLAV:
Were you depressed?

MIRJANA:
What does that mean?

TOMISLAV:
Somehow sad.

MIRJANA:
Oh, yes. That was awful. At school . . . everybody told me I had gone crazy, and they laughed at me. I didn't want to talk to anybody. In the past I had never allowed anyone to see me suffering about anything, but then after this happened to me I just wanted to sit alone, for about a fortnight. If a teacher asked me a question I

didn't know what was happening. If he spoke to me, asking why I wasn't listening, or why I didn't do anything, then I would start crying without knowing why. I was terribly sensitive. It has been really terrible. Now little by little it is easier, but it is still difficult.

TOMISLAV:
You are always thinking about her?

MIRJANA:
Oh, yes! I smile and then immediately remember that she won't come . . . I am always imposing some kind of sadness on myself. I don't exactly impose it, but I keep reminding myself that she won't come and because of that the sadness comes of itself. Something really hurts in my soul.

TOMISLAV:
During prayer, can you now experience a feeling of her presence in your inner self?

MIRJANA:
Oh, yes! I did that last night during the seven Our Fathers. I felt it beautifully, as if I were praying with her. It was as if I were hearing her voice in my heart. It was sort of echoing in me and praying with me. I didn't notice anything around me. I simply immersed myself in prayer, exactly as she does—I was hearing my voice and her voice echoing.

TOMISLAV:
Did you hear that in your ears or somewhere in your heart?

MIRJANA:
In my soul.

TOMISLAV:
What is your prayer practice now? What do you like to pray the most?

MIRJANA:
It's like this. Since I don't have her, if I go to school in the morning then in the afternoon, at the time she used to come, I go to my room and take a rosary and pray for an hour or two—depending on how much time I have; it is almost never less than an hour. I pray that God will give me strength so that I can understand normally and behave normally again. I also pray for unbelievers and their conversion and for the secrets.

TOMISLAV:
Do you like to read the Holy Scriptures?

MIRJANA:
I have the Bible, that old one; but I don't have the Holy Scriptures.

TOMISLAV:
They are the same thing.

MIRJANA:
Oh, the same thing.

TOMISLAV:
I meant the Gospel. I wondered if you read the Gospel?

MIRJANA:
Oh, there are lots of beautiful things there, really from life . . . the Bible.

TOMISLAV:
Do you read the Gospel regularly? Did anybody give you any instruction in reading the Gospel or do you read it on your own?

MIRJANA:
No, I don't. When I pray, something comes in prayer; I really immerse myself in prayer and then it comes to me as if I were speaking with someone. Then I express myself. All this is in me, talking with God. Then I go on praying again. Then again like that. I say all this out loud.

TOMISLAV:
Do you pray with someone else? Is there any prayer group there, or do you get together . . .

MIRJANA:
Mostly I am alone. Sometimes my mother comes when she is at home. She works. Then Sister Marinka. We get together to pray.

TOMISLAV:
Do you remember any other important detail from your conversations? Does any detail come to mind, let us say, from the time when you talked with Our Lady?

MIRJANA:
I really can't remember any.

TOMISLAV:
Did any healing take place around you that you know about?

MIRJANA:
Yes, in Sarajevo. There was one man who wrote and thanked me.

TOMISLAV:
What happened?

MIRJANA:
I have it all in Sarajevo. I burnt all that so that somebody . . . But I put it all down in my notebook. He was in a wheelchair and unable to walk and he wrote to me. It was a very beautiful letter, full of feeling. He told me about his suffering. Then I asked Our Lady's help for him. She said that he is a very good believer but that he should pray. He prays but not for himself. He must pray for himself, for his healing. Then he prayed. I prayed too. After three months he wrote to me saying that he had got on his feet and could walk a little with one crutch. He thanked me.

TOMISLAV:
Then Our Lady said that if you pray for a particular need . . .

MIRJANA:
Emphasize exactly that: "Dear God I am praying for my healing." You should pray for that. But you must pray from your heart, from the depths of your soul,

with feeling. It does not have to be a prayer but a conversation with God: "You see my sufferings, God. You see how I am. I'm not complaining, my cross is not difficult for me, but again I would like to be on my feet again so that I can see the world." Like that.

TOMISLAV:
How long should prayer last?

MIRJANA:
I would recommend sick people to close themselves in with God, speaking with him and praying for an hour every day. I think that this would help them very much in their souls and would bring them grace from God.

TOMISLAV:
Did you ever notice, when you asked, that Our Lady was recommending something special for some people?

MIRJANA:
She always said: "Faith, prayer, penance." She never said anything special. She always said the same thing for every sick person—never anything special. But she pointed out that it should be emphasized: I am praying for this and this and it should be prayed for with one's soul, properly. Not like: "OurFatherwhoartinheaven . . . fast. You must pray properly. The important thing is not saying the prayer, you must feel it.

TOMISLAV:
How about fasting?

MIRJANA:
She said that sick people do not have to fast. They can do some other good deed. People who can fast but who prefer doing a good deed instead of fasting—this is not enough for them, because they could fast. This only applies to people who are sick and who cannot fast because their health won't allow it.

TOMISLAV:
Does she call for everybody to fast on bread and water only, or does she allow or recommend different types of fast?

MIRJANA:
We didn't discuss it. But probably it should be bread and water only.

TOMISLAV:
For everybody?

MIRJANA:
Yes. Those who want to receive something from God, to have him help them.

TOMISLAV:
And any other detail you remember?

MIRJANA:
I don't remember anything else.

Marija, Ivanka and Jakov in back of the parish church at Medjugorje

V

Medjugorje in Context

By Robert Faricy SJ

Going again to Medjugorje

My third visit to Medjugorje took place in the autumn of 1983. Instead of going to Split or to Dubrovnik, this time I flew to Sarajevo, the largest city closest to Medjugorje. I spent the night there, took a three-hour train journey the next morning to Mostar and then a slow local bus the remaining twelve miles to Medjugorje. The bus goes right by the hotel in the small town of Citluk. During my visit, I would sleep at the Hotel Citluk, and go to and from Medjugorje on foot, a little over an hour's walk, or by taxi. But I did not want to stop now, so I went straight to the village, walked five minutes from the end of the bus line to St. James parish church and went in to pray.

In the church, I found a new addition: a large plaster statue of Our Lady, her clothing painted in the grey and white colors that the young people described as seeing her wear, on a pedestal off to the left in front of the altar rail. Several women, dressed in the somber colors of the local dress, walked slowly in a circle around the statue, saying the rosary. I prayed for a while and Father Tomislav Vlasic found me there when he came into the church early in the afternoon. He was surprised; I had not announced that I was coming. We went outside into the autumn sun and then to the presbytery-convent to talk.

Things were going on as before; nothing much had changed since my last visit. Large crowds continued to come to daily Mass, and even larger crowds on Sundays and feastdays.

Jakov's mother died recently but he still lives locally, with his uncle and aunt. A remarkable number of new houses are being built in the parish. Building permission is still denied to the Franciscans, however.

Every evening at 6:15 the church is filled for the recitation of the rosary. The young people wait for Our Lady in the auxiliary sacristy just off the sanctuary: Ivan, Vicka, Marija, Jakov and Ivanka whenever she is free from school in Mostar. Our Lady stopped appearing daily to Mirjana on Christmas Day 1982; but she was still visiting the others each evening wherever they happened to be at the time—appearing to the small group in the sacristy, and individually to anyone who could not be present there at the time. So I found myself, with several other people, mostly pilgrims like myself, in the small room waiting with the young people for Our Lady to come. The rosary began promptly at 6:15. All of us in the sacristy joined in, in low voices, praying in our own languages. The young people stood in front of the small altar-table saying the rosary like the rest of us.

Suddenly, all together, they fell silent, dropped to their knees and stared fixedly at a point not precisely on the wall but somehow beyond or within it. Our Lady had come. I stood wedged in the corner between the wall and the altar, facing the kneeling boys and girls, only feet from the nearest, Vicka. None of them fidgeted, nor for an instant moved their eyes from what they were looking at. Their expressions differed. Marija, for example, looked very calm, peaceful, reverent. Vicka was smiling and her eyes were bright. They completely ignored everything, even several exploding flashbulbs, reacting only to what they were staring at.

Sometimes one of them, most frequently Vicka, would speak to Our Lady. I could see their lips move, and even the movements of their vocal cords—especially Vicka's, because I stood so close and because she spoke, as she usually does, with animation. But I heard nothing except the drone of the rosary coming through the sacristy walls from the congregation in the church. After about fifteen minutes, the young people returned to their ordinary expressions, rose and went out of the sacristy into the sanctuary to help in leading the rosary. The rest of us remained where we were, and joined in the prayer.

I had been so close, not just to Vicka and the others, but to Our Lady herself; what did I experience? Nothing in particular. An awareness, a kind of awe at being in a holy place, present at a holy event. I had no thoughts or ideas; no words of prayer came into my head; my mind remained quite blank, peaceful and uncluttered. It felt good to be there.

After the rosary, I vested for Mass with Father Tomislav, Father Slavko—newly assigned to the parish—and several other visiting priests. As always, the Mass included a homily, several hymns sung strongly and beautifully, and a great spirit of worship, of reverent prayer, of awareness of God's presence and action and love. When the Mass ended, Fathers Slavko and Tomislav led the usual prayers for healing.

I spent the next few days in prayer. I sat long hours in the church. I visited the place on the hill near the village where Our Lady first appeared on June 24, 1981. A crude wooden cross stands there now and often a scattering of pilgrims and local people sits, stands, kneels around it in silent prayer. The spot is nearly inaccessible. I clambered uphill clumsily over rocks and through brush and I was glad to sit quietly when I arrived.

The quiet days gave me a chance to think about the events of Medjugorje, what they might mean in the context of the Church and of our present troubled times. My thoughts were not profound and not complicated. The meaning of Medjugorje is, it seems to me, quite simple.

Conversion

The meaning of Medjugorje is conversion. Jesus has sent us his mother, unexpectedly and dramatically, to wake us up, to startle us, to move us to turn our hearts to God. The message of Our Lady at Medjugorje is a call to conversion. The awful horror of war and the awful horror of sin go together. War is somehow a consequence of sin. The only way to avoid the horror of war is to turn from the horror of sin, to be converted, to turn from sin to God. The only way to peace is the way of conversion.

If I want to be converted, what can I do? How can I express my desire to turn from sin and to turn more fully to the Lord? I can reform my life; I can pray; I can fast. These activities express concretely my willingness to be converted in a fuller way and they are ways of actively participating in God's plan for the conversion of the world.

We find no new content in the message of Our Lady at Medjugorje. It is the same message that Jesus preached in his public life: "Repent and believe the gospel." It forms the heart of the Church's teaching down through the centuries. But we do find a new call, a new urgency; and this is, for each of us, a new grace, a new mercy from God.

The parallels with Fatima are striking. There are remarkable similarities between the apparitions at Medjugorje and those at the rural Portuguese village of Fatima in the spring of 1917. The message is the same: an urgent call to repentance, to pray and to do penance so as to cooperate with God's redemptive work, to avoid war and to have peace on earth. Mary told the three children at Fatima—Lucia, aged eleven and her cousins Francisco and Jacinta, aged eight and six—that unless a sufficient number of people repented and let themselves be converted, the present world war would end but another more terrible war would follow it; "another worse war will begin under Pope Pius XI." And Russia "will spread her errors throughout the world, provoking wars and persecutions of the Church."

As at Medjugorje, the children of Fatima were shown a vision of hell, to impress on them the evil of sin and of unrepentance. At both Medjugorje and Fatima, war is seen as a consequence of sin and unrepentance.

Pope John Paul II summarized the Fatima message as one that calls to repentance, gives a warning, invites to prayer and recommends the rosary. This is quite like the message of Mary at Medjugorje: conversion, warning, prayer and fasting, the rosary encouraged.

Finally both Fatima and Medjugorje faithfully bring the gospel message to bear on the contemporary world. Our Lady spoke at Fatima about the then contemporary world situation and about what would follow unless enough people repented. Over sixty years later, the world situation has changed. The Fatima prophecies have been fulfilled. We now have a new warning and a new call to conversion—in the light of present international tensions and their possible aftermath.

The Church and Medjugorje

Where does the official Church stand in regard to the events at Medjugorje? What is the attitude of the Pope, the bishops of Croatia, the local bishop?

In matters of this kind, the responsibility always remains primarily at the local level. Ordinarily, the Church begins its official investigation at the level of the diocese and depends to a great extent on the views of the local bishop. Medjugorje lies in the diocese of Mostar. One would expect the Church's first judgment on the authenticity of the Medjugorje apparitions to come from the Bishop of Mostar, basing his conclusions on the results of an officially appointed diocesan commission of investigation.

In the present case, however, the strong opposition of the Communist government and particularly of the local government considerably complicates the picture. The Bishop of Mostar finds himself confronted by a local Communist government that views all the events at Medjugorje as necessarily false because they directly contradict the official atheist ideology. The Communist government, inevitably and even necessarily (from its own point of view) sees the Franciscan priests and sisters of St. James parish as liars and the young people as naive tools manipulated by the priests for their own sinister purposes. The Bishop of Mostar is under that government, closely supervised by it, dependent on it for the necessary government approvals in matters of building, publishing, evangelizing among other matters. Were the Bishop of Mostar to approve the apparitions at Medjugorje, the government could and certainly would take severe repressive action. For instance, it could do to the bishop what it has done to other priests who have publicly shown approval of the apparitions. It could try him for sedition and send him to prison for several years without Bible or any other religious books, without being able to ever say or even to go to Mass and with all the other hardships that imprisoned priests are now suffering.

A long historical conflict between the secular clergy and the local Franciscans further complicates the situation, since Our Lady's reported apparitions are in a Franciscan parish under the jurisdiction of the bishop. For example, two young Franciscan priests have recently been accused of rebelliousness and disciplined by the bishop. Our Lady is reported to have said that the two Franciscans are innocent and that the bishop acted hastily; understandably, the bishop views the report with suspicion.

I have met the Bishop of Mostar. I am convinced that he tries to be objective with regard to events at Medjugorje, and that he is courageous in the face of possible punishment or imprisonment by the Communist authorities. But I am sure that he fears for the welfare of the people of his diocese. I met him on my way back to Sarajevo and to Rome after my third visit to Medjugorje. Having made an appointment through the Vicar General, I arrived late in the morning at the bishop's house. He invited me to stay for lunch; we talked for three hours.

Yes, the bishop assured me, he has appointed an investigating commission to look into the events at Medjugorje but as the Vicar General said to me, slowly: "There is no hurry." Nor, as far as I can see, can there be any hurry, given the opposition of the government and of the local governing authorities and the police.

In the meantime, we can hear and listen to and

cooperate with the gospel message that the Lord speaks to us. The events at Medjugorje accentuate and speak loudly that gospel message. Speaking to the six young people and through them to all of us, Our Lady gives us a message of peace and calls us to conversion, to prayer, to penance and to the sacraments of the Church.

She has promised to leave us a visible sign; this time before the visible sign is a time of grace, a time to accept conversion and to deepen our faith. The sign will be the last warning. If the world is not converted, disaster will follow.

Jesus, speaking to us through his mother, calls us with great urgency. What can we do? We can renounce our sins and be sorry for them. We can turn to the Lord.

VI
Later Events

By Lucy Rooney SND

June 24 and 25, 1984, the third anniversary of Our Lady's appearing at Medjugorje, and her feast day as Mary Queen of Peace. I was among the more than ten thousand pilgrims converging on the church of St. James. The police did not facilitate our journey. We were stopped at the crossroads leading to the village; passports were examined, bags searched very thoroughly. Some buses were turned away. Passengers from other buses were made to walk the last few kilometers, even though they included sick pilgrims. Those who were camping in tents near the church were turned out except for the intrepid priests from Cork who confounded the police by speaking only Irish! They went back to their sleeping bags. I saw two camping trailers and a dozen buses which had been allowed through. There were few private cars.

So many pilgrims came from overseas that Masses were said each day in Italian, German, French and English, as well as Croatian. The majority of people were from Yugoslavia itself. They came on foot with no plans to stay anywhere, carrying what they would need for a night or two in the open. Even after a hot day, the mountain wind is cold at night, so the church was left open all night so that all could pray or sleep. It was a rather amusing mixture of both—everyone respecting the other's decision.

Most of the pilgrims climbed the 1800 feet to the cross on the mountain, and to Podbrdo Hill, to the site of the first apparition. As we climbed, I saw many elderly people carrying their possessions, and many young and not so young who were barefooted on the sharp flint rock. All were praying. It was this continual prayer at Medjugorje which touched me most—the response to Our Lady's urging to "Pray, pray, pray."

Medjugorje is still unspoiled but still without facilities such as toilets. A booth was selling soft drinks and coffee, to supplement the single water tap. A few beggars have moved in, displaying their maimed limbs until the police move them on, not unkindly. I found the winemaking room, where the children have their catechism, transformed into a bright classroom, the vats removed, the floor retiled.

There are still just four priests and three sisters; but for this weekend, every Franciscan priest and sister who could get away had come to help. So I met two main characters of the Medjugorje story: Father Jozo Krizic and Father Jozo Zovko, the former pastor. The parishioners greeted them with great joy. These two Fathers Jozo, both recently released from prison, impressed me by their remarkable joy. It was a joy of a special quality. I asked Father Jozo Krizic about his time in solitary without any books. For six months, he was sick but was not allowed to see a doctor, until eventually a petition reached the commissioner. He worked during his thirty months imprisonment in a furniture factory. The noise of the drills has damaged his hearing permanently. His crime? An article written about the reported apparitions. His editor, Father Ferdo Vlasic, now aged 64 years, has still five years to serve in jail. Father Krizic said that he prayed every moment of those thirty months. When asked if he experienced spiritual joy in prison, his face lit up, and he raised his arms above his head, saying "spiritual joy!" But when we asked him if Our Lady had visited him, he was embarrassed to answer—he did not want to say "Yes," but could not say "No"; "to Jozo Kovko," he said laughing.

Father Tomislav Vlasic told me that the apparitions continue daily. They are usually brief. Mirjana, who no longer has daily visions, saw Our Lady on March 18, 1983 and 1984 (Mirjana's birthday). On the second occasion, Our Lady remained thirteen minutes. She urged Mirjana on the spiritual life and told her to remember the secrets. Before leaving, she said to Mirjana, "This year probably we will see each other again on account of the secrets." Mirjana knows all ten secrets, Vicka eight, and the others nine.

Have there been any new developments? Yes. The Blessed Virgin has been speaking and appearing frequently to a twelve year-old girl, Jelena Vasilj, apart from the regular daily apparitions to the young people in the small room in the church. The words and appearances to Jelena take the form of clear interior locutions, words spoken by Mary to Jelena and heard interiorly by Jelena, and visions of Our Lady. At first it seemed that what Our Lady said to Jelena was only for her and, sometimes for the people of the local parish. Later, however, some of the revelations to Jelena have had a more universal character.

Most importantly, Our Lady has sent a message to "the Pope and to Christians," giving the exact date of her birthday, and asking everyone to prepare before, for three days. (It was two thousand years ago in the summer of this year, 1984.) Mary said, "Throughout the centuries I have dedicated my entire life for you. Is it too much for you to dedicate three days for me? Don't do any work on that day, but take your rosaries in your hands and pray." Our Lady asked for the three days of preparation to be days of fasting and prayer. She said there will be "great conversions." The message was sent to Pope John Paul and to Bishop Pavao Zanic of Mostar. The Bishop did not want the date to be revealed beforehand unless Pope John Paul announced it.

Another development concerns the Commission of Inquiry set up by the Bishop of Mostar. The Commission is now enlarged to twenty members. Most of them visited Medjugorje on May 24. Two teams of doctors, one from Milan and one from Montpellier have examined the children and found heart and brain to be normal. All agreed that during the apparitions the young people are living outside space and time. One of the members of the Commission pricked Vicka three times with a needle, drawing blood. This episode was filmed by Portuguese television. Vicka made no sign, and continued to smile radiantly at Our Lady.

At Mary's request, the parishioners of Medjugorje meet once a week to pray together and to be instructed by Our Lady. The young people of the parish have a prayer group too. Our Lady has said through Mirjana, "I have chosen this parish in a special way. I want to protect you and guide you in love. And therefore I ask for a total conversion of the parish so that the pilgrims can find a fountain of conversion here." She recommended particularly adoration of the Blessed Sacrament and veneration of the wounds of Jesus. Our Lady has asked them that on the day they meet, they read in the presence of the Blessed Sacrament (or if this is not possible, then in their families), a passage from the Gospel of Matthew, chapter six, verses 24 to 34. She suggested that they should give up, on this day, some pleasure, such as cigarettes or alcohol; those who are more generous should fast.

During Holy Week 1984, Our Lady said to them, through Jelena, "Raise your hands and open your hearts. Now, in the moment of the resurrection, Jesus wants to give you a particular gift. This gift of my Son is my gift, it is this: You will undergo trials with great ease. We will be nearby and will show you the way out if you will accept us. Don't say that the Holy Year is now over and there is no more need to pray. On the contrary, reinforce your prayers, because the Holy Year is just one step forward." After this, Jelena saw the risen Jesus. Brilliant light radiated from his wounds onto the people. Jesus said, "Receive my graces and tell the whole world there will be happiness only through me."

About prayer, Our Lady has instructed the people

through Marija and Jelena. To Jelena Mary said, "I know that every family can pray four hours each day." Jelena responded: "But if I tell this to the people they may back out." Our Lady replied, "Even you don't understand. It is only one-sixth of the day." "I know that you want us to pray continuously," said Jelena.

Father Vlasic says that on holy days as many as forty parishioners will come to church to spend the whole day in prayer. They have learned the meaning of resting in the Lord on Sundays and holy days.

Our Lady has explained: "When I say 'pray, pray, pray,' I don't mean only increase the hours of prayer, but increase the desire to pray and to be in contact with God, to be in a continuous prayerful state of mind."

On Holy Thursday 1984, Our Lady sent a message through Jelena: "I will show you a spiritual secret: if you want to be stronger than evil, make an active conscience for yourself. That is, pray a reasonable amount in the morning, read a text of holy scripture, and plant the divine word in your heart, and try to live it during the day, especially in moments of trial. So you will be stronger than evil." Our Lady has also indicated that peace, which is the heart of her message, is needed for prayer. She has said that peace should be present before prayer and during prayer, and that prayer should conclude with peace and reflection. This peace is a happiness which comes from dialogue with God.

Father Tomislav Vlasic was asked about the signs. His opinion is that some of these signs, these warnings, are near. For example, Our Lady told Marija that they might see each other again this year on account of the secrets. But, he says, "I have learned during these three years that one cannot consider the messages and the secrets in a logical way, according to human standards, nor in a mathematical way; the dynamic is different."

Our Lady has said that she will leave a permanent, visible sign at the site of the first apparitions. Recently a priest who is a water diviner thought that he detected two powerful streams of waters, underground. As they converge, they will burst out at the surface. The police heard of his activities on the hillside and took Father Tomislav Vlasic in for two hours of questioning.

The signs at Medjugorje continue. "All these signs are to strengthen your faith," says Our Lady. Many who were outside the church on June 24, 1984 saw the sun spinning during the moments of the apparition of the Madonna to the five children. I myself saw the sun spinning just as Mass was beginning on June 25, 1984, about 7:05 p.m. (6:05 by the sun's time). No one was excited; a few people were pointing to the sun. The phenomenon lasted about five minutes. I could look right into the sun which appeared to be a flat disc, off-white in color, spinning rapidly. From time to time light pulsed out from behind the disc. I tried to see if my blinking coincided with these pulsations of fire, but it was not so. I found that I could look away without my eyes being dazzled. Afterwards, the sun returned to its normal brilliance, and for the next hour, before it set, I could no longer look at it directly.

But that is not what one wants to say on returning from Medjugorje. The message is peace, peace through changing our lives. Recently, Our Lady has given two messages which can help us to peace. The first is for our everyday lives: "If you want to be very happy, live a simple life, humble, pray a lot, and don't worry and fret over your problems—let them be settled by God."

The second message concerns our attitude toward the future. Jelena had been reading an article about the third secret of Fatima. Our Lady said to her, "Don't think about wars, chastisements, evil. It is when you concentrate on these things that you are on the way to enter into them. Your responsibility is to accept divine peace, to live it."

Ivan, Marija, Jakov and Vicka